BREATH BY BREATH

BREATH BY BREATH

poems of guru arjan

nanak shabads

translated from the original

Sushil Rao

This book was joyfully printed
by the generous support of **Elizabeth Rao**
who not only provided the funds for its printing
but also shares her life, love, heart
and inspiration with me everyday.

Thank you for taking such good care of us Eliza
i adore you

---

in Celebration of Life !
in the loving care of a Living Master !
Clarity without Explanations !

Breath by Breath
isbn : **0-9679187-9-0**

---

sushilgrao@gmail.com

Guru Puja 2012 - Europe edition - 100 copies

---

hrdaipress
new york : miami
754 246 8787

dedicated

to those who appreciate life

breath by breath

From the beginning of time the thirsty have looked for water and the one who knew where that water was has looked for the thirsty. Somehow they have found each other and enjoyed. It is an ancient game, and the success of this game is well documented. It happens because we have thirst. Thirst is what makes us recognize the value of water. When we are not thirsty we'll walk past any amount of water but when we are thirsty we'll walk miles for a small quantity. When we discover the thirst of the heart something wonderful becomes possible.

Every Master has pointed out where that water is. That is how people recognized that he was a Master. But not everybody recognized him while he was alive. He was not walking around with a halo over his head. Many smart, educated people did not recognize him meeting him face to face. Most people mistook him for an ordinary person. The only ones who recognized were those who came to him with a thirst to know. Only those who became satisfied understood. Some called it heaven, some called it God, some called it peace, but they all said they found it within. The day we find this place called `within' is truly the day of our success as human beings.

This book is a collection of poems by those who found what they were searching for. Except for that experience everything is speculation and guesswork. That experience is beyond imagination and beyond communication. It has to be felt. One does not understand truth and then start feeling it. One feels it first and then starts to understand. I don't know of anyone who achieved this without the help of a Master.

I have such a Master. The kindness of my Master is that he not only pointed out where that water is but he also provided me with superb tools and active support that has helped me immensely. His caring has no substitute. It is what makes success possible and the journey very enjoyable. Make every effort to tune in with the living Master of your time. It is the most wonderful thing that can happen to you.

POEMS OF GURU ARJAN

with every breath

har praan prabhoo sukh daate

with every breath
God is giving
by Master's kindness
some recognize

your saints are so
beloved to you
death can never
defeat them

colored by you
they shine bright
full of the feeling
of holiness

all sins, aches
and diseases disappear
with one glimpse
of God's reality

asleep or awake
i sing his praises
Nanak worships
his Master's voice

the opportunity

bhaee paraapat maanukh dehureeaa

having obtained
this human body
this is your opportunity
to meet your lifegiver

all other strife
is useless
find holy company
and focus within

make an effort
to transcend the world
life goes wasted
chasing illusions

focus, discipline and love
i have not earned
how to worship and serve God
i don't know

Nanak says
my deeds are lowly
please keep dignity
of a shelter seeker

why neglect

maatee te jin saajiaa

why neglect the one
who created this unique body
out of sheer dust
and covered all blemishes
to make it look beautiful

why ignore the one within
who has such wonderful qualities
rejecting God he who involves
with everything else
ends up mingling with dust

experience God breath by breath
don't procrastinate
ignore the world
involve with God
let go bad connections

he who made many out of one
and gave them different colors
exists now and will always exist
learn Master's way
and serve God

higher than the highest
vast and immense
present in everyone's heart
please accept Nanak
as a servant of your servants

no judgement

hamree ganat na ganeeaa kaaee

our accounts
he does not keep
recognize
in your heart

with his hand
he sustains us as his
always always
feel his love

our beloved creator
is very forgiving
i found union
by Master's kindness

he who designed
our life and body
and gave us things
to wear and eat
he himself takes care
of his creatures

of him
Nanak is in awe

whose everything is

jis kaa sab kich tis kaa hoyi

whose everything is
become his
such a person
carries no debt

God's servant
is always free
what God gives
he accepts
a servant's lifestyle
is utterly simple
leaving everything
he turns to God
how can maya
touch such a person
he whose heart is filled
with love of God
for him no worries
even in dreams

Nanak met
his perfect Master
who dispelled
his delusions

wine of illusions

kaam krodh ahankaar vigoote

desires, frustrations and ego
make things worse
seekers escape
by turning within

drunk on the wine of illusions
fools remain asleep
seekers stay awake
enjoying within

deluded by desires
fools run around
seekers stay centered
on the love within

attached to a rat hole
fools call it home
liberated saints
reside in God's world

Nanak, everybody
who comes to God
becomes filled
with joy

the true helper

vaido na vaaee bhaino na bhaaee

not doctors
not friends
not sisters
not brothers
only God
is our true helper

his will
is what happens
he is the one
who erases
the sins of all
who turn to him

the one who is everywhere
who dwells in every heart
whose reality is eternal
who doesn't come and go
who accompanies us always
whose kindness is total
who cares for his devotees
whom the saints love
that giver of life
that source of everything

with such a God
Nanak is in love

this beautiful consciousness

santaa kee hoyi daas ree

become a servant of saints
learn their way of life
the noblest of all qualities
do not think God is far

this beautiful consciousness of ours
color it with God's love
let go cleverness and cunning
experience God's nearness

accept beloved's kindness
let this be your grooming
forget other attractions
enjoy inner sweetness

let Master's words be your lamp
make yourself a bed of truth
all day long keep hands joined
you will meet your beloved

do all grooming for him
God's beauty is unique
Nanak, she is a real bride
who pleases her husband

those who ignore

jinee naam visaariaa

those who
ignore God
them i have seen
becoming dust

children friends
house and wife
these connections
come to an end

o my mind
turn to God constantly

you will not burn
in the ocean of flames
be filled with peace
in mind and body

as a tree's shadow
disappears
when the wind
brings clouds

devote yourself
to God
meet Master
he will help you

if you stay asleep

soyi rahee prabh khabar na jaanee

if you stay asleep
and don't realize God
when morning comes
you will despair

find your God
within yourself now
if you want to succeed
don't be lazy

in your hands
is a cup of nectar
don't be careless
and let it spill

if arrogance
brings you suffering
don't blame God
for your problems

the darkness
of ignorance ends
in the light
of Knowledge

this is how Nanak
found his beloved

he who is focused

jaa kee raam naam liv laagee

he whose love
is focused on God
only that self inspired person
can be called truly blessed

free of evil
detached from illusions
having let go the poison of ego
he depends on the God in his heart

he sleeps worryless
awakens worryless
lives worryless
and laughs with detachment

Nanak, that maya
who cheats the whole world
is cheated
by servants of God

all joys

sarab sukhaa guru charnaa

all joys are found
in Master's presence

he washes away all evil
he clarifies the mind
with his help
i reach across

worship, adoration,
service and prayer
this is the effort
worth making always

heart blossoms
clarity happens
never again have to
endure confusion

observe of the saints
their peaceful face
this is the practise
to do

God towards Nanak
became kind and gracious
he gave him the shelter
of the living Master's feet

heart's salvation

guru ke charan jeea kaa nistaaraa

heart's salvation
lies in Master's hands
who can take it across
in an instant

some believe in rituals
some go to holy places
Nanak focuses
on the giver of life

the real God
severs all bonds
Nanak adores
the God within

everyone's lifegiver

too daataa jeeaa sabnaa kaa

beloved giver
of everyone's life
please come
and dwell in me

the heart in
which you reside
confusion and darkness
cannot come near

whenever i turn to you
you are there

with such kindness
you take care of everything
you have my
constant admiration

breath by breath
i cherish your love
your love is all
i want

Nanak found
his creator's support
other longings
became obsolete

hear me my friend

sun yaar hamaare sajan

hear me my friend
i have a desperate need
for my beloved's love
i am wandering searching

to that sweet person
who can put me in touch
even for one instant
i offer my head

my eyes are addicted
to seeing my beloved
without him
they are never still

my heart
is linked to God
like a fish to water
like a rainbird to rain

when seeker Nanak
met his Master
all his burning
ended

ask God

maango raam te ik daan

i ask of God
one gift only

all my wishes will be fulfilled
if you teach me your name

may your feet
reside in my heart

may i always find
company of your saints

may my mind
not get stuck in sorrow

may i sing your praises
twenty four hours a day

at all times serving God
at all hours focusing within

Nanak is colored in God's color
no birth nor death again

such a kindness

aisee kirpaa mohe karo

such a blessing
do for me

let a saint's feet
rest on my head
let my eyes see him
let his dust fall on me

let his words
settle in my heart
let God's name
reside in my mind

please protect me
from the five thieves
burn all my doubts
in fire of knowing

what you give
that i accept
please free me
from fantasy

Nanak's lord
only you can give
please enrich me
with holy company

beloved come home

mohan ghari aavo karo jodareeaa

beloved come home
i beg of you

i act in pride
i speak arrogantly
i am mistake prone
but i am yours

i know you are near
but i can't perceive
wandering deluded
i am filled with sorrow

becoming gracious
Guru removed veil
meeting beloved
heart blossomed

one moment
if i forget
feels like a
million years

when he found
a gathering of saints
Nanak became
intimate with God

those who focus

jin har har naam dhiaayaa

those who focus
on God's love
attain all joys

where there is
a hunger for holiness
there one's whole life
becomes focused

whoever practices
Master's teaching
rises beyond sorrow

those seekers
are true saints
who don't focus
on others' faults

divine is their Master
who placed the
sweet fruit of God
in their mouth

those who serve

jin jan gurumukh seveaa

those who serve
attain all joys

they themselves succeed
and help everybody else

they become rich
in God's love

they let go worldly greed
and find love within

always always
happiness in their home

God becomes
their friend and helper

they treat their enemies
as they treat their friends

with everyone
they are always fair

only he is happy in this world
who meditates on Knowledge

i experienced what was written
in ancient times

and found my harmony
with God

life of the saints

har har sant janaa kee jeevan

God is
the life of saints
external pleasures
are like poison to them
they drink holiness
from the ocean of joy

gather the priceless
jewels of holiness
and sew them into
your mind and body
colored by God
let mind became divine
enjoy the intoxication
of holiness

like fish that depend on water
depend on God's love
Nanak, saints, like rainbirds,
crave only drops of God's love

sit still at home

thir ghar baiso hari jan pyaare

sit still at home
beloved of God
your Master shall fulfill
your heart

God destroys
the agents of evil
the creator preserves
his servant's honor

kings and emperors
are in his control
he provides supreme love
and immortality

becoming fearless
focus on God
gather in holy company
accept his gift

taking shelter
of the omnipresent God
Nanak drinks
supreme being's love

focus within

guru kee moorat man me dhyaano

focus on Master's image within
keep his words alive in your mind

install his feet in your heart
he is the One everyone prays to

don't neglect and get lost in the world
nobody gets across without a guide

Master shows lost ones the way home
he brings one to the experience of God

he frees us from the terror of death
his generosity is priceless and without end

all who succeeded learnt it from him
he awakens the sleeping heart

by his gift the inner lotus blossoms
where it is dark he brings light

he is the doer, he is capable
he is the architect of the universe

this is what Master taught Nanak
no liberation without learning

extremely capable

guru parmesar karnaihaar

the living Master is extremely capable
he is the lord of the universe

he is the one
keeping everything in place

by meditating on him
all sorrows depart

if you are drowning in the world
he can pull you out

what is broken
he can join

serve him night and day
with trust and joy

peace will come to you
of its own accord

only the very fortunate
receive Master's blessing

Nanak admires his kindness
and dedicates forever

desert winds

taatee vaao na lagaee paarbrahm saranaaee

desert winds do not come near the one
who has taken God's shelter

he has God's protection from all sides
sorrow cannot approach

i met my perfect Master
who revealed the secret to me

he gave me the medicine of God's name
and gathered my focus in one place

my creator takes care of me
and all my sorrows are erased

Nanak's blessing has happened
God himself has become my helper

Master's love

maaee charan guru meethe

mother
Master's love is sweet

great blessing God gives
meeting Master brings a million joys

hearing the praises of the imperishable
desires and frustrations start to leave

experiencing reality
death does not bother

without God all attractions are empty
i realized by Master's kindness

Nanak found the jewel of the heart
without which one departs cheated

contentment

maayi mere man ko sukh

mother, contentment
has come to my heart

infinite bliss, royal happiness
he lets me enjoy

by focusing on God
all sorrows disappear

millions of sins are erased
body and mind feel good

seeing his reality
hope becomes fulfilled

one glimpse
and hunger subsides

with God, all treasures, powers
and magic wands become real

Nanak found refuge in the ocean of joy
and escaped suffering forever

obeying Master

guru guru karat sadaa sukh paayaa

following Master
i found my lasting joy

the helper of the needy
became kind to me

he gave me Knowledge
and taught me to see

in his holy company
i found my holiness

drinking God's love
my heart became fulfilled

i found my joy
awaiting me within

Nanak succeeded
by singing God's praises

become one

saach naam meraa man laagaa

my heart has experienced
the holiness of God
my interactions with people
has become simple

on the outside
i mix with everyone
inside, i am detached
like a lotus

with everybody, i use
the language of words
with God, i speak
with my heart

outside
i seem fierce
inside, i am a servant
of his children

Nanak found
his perfect Master
inside and outside
became one

love has happened

moo laalan sio preet banee

for me
love with God
has happened

breaking
does not break it
leaving
does not leave it

such a knot
beloved has tied

day and night
within my heart
he is always present
our lifegiver
is very kind to us

i am in awe
of the one i love
whose untellable story
i have grasped

begs Nanak
the servant of your servants
please keep me
in your love

your union

aape mayl laye

you are the one
who brought union

ever since i came to you
regrets disappeared

secure in your care
anxiety vanished

by practicing Knowledge
my body has healed

you have saved
even the most ignorant fools

when Nanak met his Master
lostness ended

my support

prabh jee too mere praan adhaarai

beloved God
you are the support
of my lifebreath

salutations prostrations prayers
i surrender myself many times
standing sitting asleep or awake
my mind is thinking of you

joy sorrow heart's loneliness
all are in your sight
you are my support strength
wisdom wealth and family

what you do
is for my good
Nanak is happy
seeing God's feet

you are infinite

too be-ant ko birlaa jaane

you are without limits
very few realize
by Master's kindness
some discover your secret

your servant's longing
beloved, is to live
at your feet
and experience God

kind being
holy giver
those to whom you reveal
to them the secret is known

always always
i dedicate myself
wherever i look
i see your kindness

i am virtueless
i have no skills
coming to Master
Nanak's heart rejoices

God of joy

niranjan maalaa

the true rosary
is in the heart
turning night and day
by itself

it goes up it goes down
each breath appears and disappears
nobody observes this
wasting time on useless things

the inner rosary
is counted without fingers
sleeping or awake
that counting never stops

the inner chant
goes on and on
Master reveals the techniques
that lead to peace

whoever meditates regularly
becomes free

in whose heart

jaa ke hirdai vaseaa too karte

in whose heart you reside, o creator
fear and longing are all resolved
you never abandon your servant
dust from your feet blesses his heart

your untellable story
cannot be told
source of all good
dear happiness giving God

a human being is
what you allow him to be
to your servant you give service
seeing you he feels inspired

within, he sees your oneness
to whom you gave Guru's gift
their ignorance ended
and you became real

he knows he is focused
he is the human ideal
says Nanak, to whom he is kind
from his heart never forgotten

eyes cleansed

netra puneet bhaye daras pekhe

my eyes have cleansed
upon seeing.
holy dust
has fallen on my head

with great joy
i sing God's praises
my life-giver resides
in my heart

you are my sustainer
my beautiful, wise
and infinite father
you are extremely kind

very beautiful and joy-creating
manifestations you have
your words
are so rich

with his feet
in his heart
Nanak is tied
to Master's teaching

heavenly joy

raaj leelaa tere naam banaaee

heavenly joy
your Knowledge brings
union happens
i sing your praises

all happiness
found in your shelter
Master lifts
the veil of not-knowing

understanding his vision
i celebrate with joy
serving Master
is very liberating

householder or monk
whoever knows you
by practising Knowledge
becomes instantly free

whoever finds
the treasure of Knowledge
Nanak, his treasure chest
becomes full

the real God

oothat sukheeaa baithat sukheeaa

the giver of life
is the real God
the one who lives
in every heart

happy standing
happy sitting
enjoy life
free of fear

sleep in peace
wake up free
wherever you look
God is present

happy at home
happy outside
my beloved Master
opened my eyes

never dies

naa oh martaa naa ham dariaa

he never dies so i never fear
he never disappears so i never grieve
he is never poor so i am never needy
he is never sad so i am never lonely

there is no other causer of death
in our heart lives the giver of life

he has no ties so i am not bound
he has no trade so i have no debts
he has no dirt so i stay clean
he is all bliss so i am full of joy

he has no worries so i have no stress
he has no stains so i don't need cleaning
he has no hunger i have no desires
where he is pure there i admire

i am nothing he is everything
in the past and future he alone exists
Master erased all Nanak's doubts
he and i met and became one color

God's love

prabh kee preet sadaa sukh hoye

God's love is always enjoyable
God's love never brings pain
God's love washes dirt of ego
God's love is always pure

listen friend such is God's love
to every heart he gives life-support

God's love all treasures
God's love satisfies the heart
God's love is always attractive
God's love resolves all problems

God's love transcend the world
God's love no fear of death
God's love prospers everything
God's love goes wherever you go

by oneself
one neither finds nor gets lost
he who is blessed
is attracted to holiness

Nanak
is dedicated to you
your love is
the support of your lovers

in harmony with God

thakur sio jaa kee ban aaee

those who are
in harmony with God
are enjoying life fully
they journey satisfied

for those who serve God
in eating spending
enjoying and sharing
nothing is lacking

for those who have
a limitless provider
how can shortage
come near

whom worship
all the saints
a glimpse of him
and fall in love

upon whom
God's grace falls
exists not for them
any lack

he feeds everybody

apnee ukat khalaave bhojan

he feeds each one
as he chooses
he plays with us
when he wants

he provides us
with comfort, toys and love
he keeps himself
always near us

our father
the giver of our life
is very kind to us
he nurtures us
as a mother her child

friend and well-wisher
expert in everything
he is the always
thankable God

present here
there and everywhere
Nanak found God
by serving Master

love, bliss and joy

aanad rang binod hamaare

love, bliss and joy
fill my life

praising holiness
experiencing holiness
holiness is the source
of my life

holiness is wisdom
holiness is purification
God's holiness
fulfills my purpose

holiness is beauty
holiness is greatness
God's holiness carries me
across the worldly ocean

the sorrowless, priceless
jewel of holiness
i received
at my Master's feet

God is very kind
to Nanak
his heart became content
seeing a glimpse of him

bliss occurred

sagal ichh meree puneeaa

all my wishes came true
i found my invisible lifegiver

bliss occurred, i felt very blessed
God came and manifested at home

love came home by previous earnings
who can measure love's greatness

limitless, perfect, giver of all joys
how can tongue describe

he brought union, hugged me close
without his help, i could not reach

Nanak, dedicate and serve
God is present within everyone

breath by breath

tis guru ko simro saas saas

i love my Master
breath by breath
Master is my life
Master is my wealth

seeing my Master i come alive
i wash his feet and drink
i bathe daily in Master's dust
who washes away the dirt of ego

for my Master i swing a fan
who saved me with his own hand
for my Master i fetch water
who taught me clarity

for my Master i grind corn
who makes enemies into friends
my Master gave me life
and made me his slave by purchase

he himself offered his love
i bow to him with gratitude
for resolving all my doubts
Nanak's Master is supremely kind

since the moment

jab te darsan bhete saadhoo

since the moment i met my Master
my good days arrived
always happy always praising
i found the one who loves

now for me
my heart sings of God's love
clarity and peace in my heart
i have found my savior

when the source of good rules the heart
sadness, confusion and fear run away
the invisible thing becomes found
the color of holiness becomes permanent

free of anxiety thoughts still
regret, greed and attachments disappear
disease of ego subsides
by his kindness fear of death leaves

Master's wishes, Master's service
and Master's directions become attractive
Nanak is dedicated
to the one who frees from death

my Master cares

satguru apnaa sad sadaa samhaare

my Master is always
taking care of me
i wipe his feet
with my hair

wake up mind
now is the time
without God
life is empty

align yourself
with Master's teaching
what Master gives
makes sorrow disappear

other than Master
there is nowhere to go
Master is the only one
offering Knowledge

Master is supreme being
the lord of the universe
twenty four hours a day
Nanak turns to Master

Master's message

mere man sabad laago guru meethaa

Master's message
is sweet to my ears

my destiny has awakened
my dawn has arrived

the real God dwells
in every heart

beyond everything
self-existing, accessible to all

Master revealed to me
God's eternal name

i surrendered
my heart to him

the dust of holiness
has fallen on my head

my search has ended
in success

Nanak has become colored
in the color of God's love

neediness is soothed

trisnaa bujhe har ke naame

neediness is soothed
by the experience of God

contentment is found
in Master's words

it becomes possible
to focus on God

the spell of illusion lifted
when Master became kind

he revealed to me God's name
by meditating on it i live

servant's wishes
all became fulfilled

joy, peace and endless love
are in the heart

in whose destiny it is written
he finds God's love

servant Nanak's efforts
became fruitful

as you wish

soee karaaye jo tudh bhaave

have me do
what you want
of cleverness
i know nothing

i am a child
in your care
you yourself
take care of me

you are my mother
and my father

with great kindness
you nurture me
all that happens
is by your will

all living creatures
depend on you
my leash is
in your hands

have me do
what you want
Nanak is a servant
in your care

a note on the translation

I have attempted to keep things as simple as possible. These poems are loyal to the originals but not literal. I have tried to focus on the feeling rather than the words. In the interests of simplicity, I have dropped a lot of the old-Hindi terminology and tried to see the poems in a universal light. I left out punctuation and capitals except where necessary.

I work as a poet, not a scholar, and these poems are inspirations, not explanations. I want to draw attention, not to the poems or the poets, but to the experience they talk about.

I know these poems mainly as songs. They are the gospel and folk music of India. There are thousands of such songs floating around, in different languages, composed by different saint-poets. I find them very inspiring and they never get old. Each song is unique. Each has its own tune (raga), rhythm, mood, etc. Each is unforgettable and grows and evolves in my mind. As time passes, they are yielding newer and deeper insights and are becoming more and more intimate.

I love listening to them.

acknowledgements

Many people helped in making this book possible, without whose support it would have been much harder to finish. I thank each of you who helped. You know who you are. A big hug to the spirit of the poets for composing these beautiful long-lived poems. Many of them have been enjoyed for centuries and are still wonderful and powerful to listen to. I also wish to thank all the musicians who perform these songs for keeping them fresh and alive.

But most of all, I want to thank my Master, Maharaji, (www.WOPG.org) for awakening my heart and giving me Knowledge. He has taught me simplicity and led me to the natural joy within. He has breathed life into my devotion and made it real. He continues to guide me in my daily life and helps me keep this fire burning. He reminds me again and again of what is important. I am benefitting immensely from what he is doing. I could never have translated these poems without his inspiration. These poems are more his than mine. I am very grateful for this privilege.

All the time I was working on this book I was very aware of my great fortune. It felt as if Kabir and the other poets were standing on one side, whispering their poems in my ears, and my Master was standing on the other, laughing and unlocking their mystery. Without the inner experience that my Master taught me, these poems would have been mere speculations. But because of what he has done for me they have become real and I can relate to them as an experience and not just a nice idea. Based on what has happened for me I have great hopes for all of mankind. I think peace is not only possible, it is imminent! Many people will find peace within themselves, not as a group, but as individuals. It is already happening. I have seen it with my own eyes. My Master can help everybody. I have total confidence in his purpose and ability.

We are very lucky to have him.

Come and listen to him speak.

other books of poetry

The Thirsty Fish
Poems of Kabir

The Want of the Heart
Poems of Mira

The Sanctuary Within
Poems of Guru Nanak

The Inner Staircase
Poems of Brahmanand

Trap the Trapper
Poems of Bhagat Kabir

Breath by Breath
Poems of Guru Arjan

Seeing Without Eyes
Poems of Finding

Feel Your Thirst
Poems of Quest

Beloved, May I Enter
Kabir Dohas

Beloved, May I Stay
Kabir Dohas

US $ 16.00

Pay securely by **PayPal** to
sushilgrao@gmail.com

please e-mail me to send a Money Order
(US $ only) - sorry, no checks.

Free Shipping within the continental US.
International orders please add $4.00 per book

---

sushilgrao@gmail.com
new york : miami
754 246 8787
hrdaipress.com

dedicated

to those who appreciate life

breath by breath

From the beginning of time the thirsty have looked for water and the one who knew where that water was has looked for the thirsty. Somehow they have found each other and enjoyed. It is an ancient game, and the success of this game is well documented. It happens because we have thirst. Thirst is what makes us recognize the value of water. When we are not thirsty we'll walk past any amount of water but when we are thirsty we'll walk miles for a small quantity. When we discover the thirst of the heart something wonderful becomes possible.

Every Master has pointed out where that water is. That is how people recognized that he was a Master. But not everybody recognized him while he was alive. He was not walking around with a halo over his head. Many smart, educated people did not recognize him meeting him face to face. Most people mistook him for an ordinary person. The only ones who recognized were those who came to him with a thirst to know. Only those who became satisfied understood. Some called it heaven, some called it God, some called it peace, but they all said they found it within. The day we find this place called `within' is truly the day of our success as human beings.

This book is a collection of poems by those who found what they were searching for. Except for that experience everything is speculation and guesswork. That experience is beyond imagination and beyond communication. It has to be felt. One does not understand truth and then start feeling it. One feels it first and then starts to understand. I don't know of anyone who achieved this without the help of a Master.

I have such a Master. The kindness of my Master is that he not only pointed out where that water is but he also provided me with superb tools and active support that has helped me immensely. His caring has no substitute. It is what makes success possible and the journey very enjoyable. Make every effort to tune in with the living Master of your time. It is the most wonderful thing that can happen to you.